Women
Code Of Conduct

Women Code Of Conduct
Copyright © 2024 by Mouna M. Fall

Published in the United States of America

Library of Congress Control Number: 2024900460
ISBN   Paperback: 979-8-89091-780-5
ISBN   eBook: 979-8-89091-781-2

All rights reserved. No part of this publication may be reproduced, stored in a retrieval system or transmitted in any way by any means, electronic, mechanical, photocopy, recording or otherwise without the prior permission of the author except as provided by USA copyright law.

The opinions expressed by the author are not necessarily those of ReadersMagnet, LLC.

ReadersMagnet, LLC
10620 Treena Street, Suite 230
San Diego, California, 92131 USA
1.619. 354. 2643 | www.readersmagnet.com

Book design copyright © 2024 by ReadersMagnet, LLC. All rights reserved.

Cover design by Jhiee Oraiz
Interior design by Don De Guzman

Women
Code Of Conduct

Mouna M. Fall

PREFACE

Every woman should have one of these.

"I am a woman, phenomenally. Phenomenal woman, that's me." Maya Angelou said it so well!

Women are phenomenal and we should never let anyone or anything make us think otherwise. Often we believe that to be considered a woman is to pass a certain age, to be married or have children. Some other times we believe that being a woman is to be able to display a certain level of maturity, attitude or personality.

Society has its pack of prejudgemental ideas on how to get the title of a woman. A transgender woman may not be accepted as a woman because her birth gender is different from the female gender. A single young female may not be given the woman title because she does not qualify for all sorts of expectations. Regardless of all the fake news, as women, we know who we are, and we are simply phenomenal, beautifully made creatures who are conquering the world striving and winning.

Let me share some research on the importance of wolves in the ecosystem by using the Yellowstone National Park. I believe this example portrays how important women are in society. So during a period of time between 1926 and 1995 without wolves, this habitat changed drastically. The population of elk, no longer pressured by predatory wolves, became abundant and began to damage their own habitat. Having lost the fear of being hunted, elk gathered near streams, overbrowsing aspens, willows, cottonwoods, and shrubs that grow on banks and prevent erosion. They wore down these areas, thus habitat for fish, amphibians, and reptiles declined as waters became broader, shallower, and warmer without shade from streamside vegetation. Elk populations were so out of control that park rangers began to kill and relocate elk in large numbers in an attempt to reduce their burgeoning population.

Aspens seldom reach full height in Yellowstone's northern valleys. Having been browsed by elk, the new sprouts and shoots were eaten, and existing trees were stunted. Along streams and around wetlands, willows and cottonwoods were also not regenerating as effectively under heavy browsing pressure from elk. Fewer young trees meant songbirds lost nesting space. Beaver populations decreased as they rely on this vegetation to survive. At one point, only one beaver colony was living in the park! Coyotes, no longer having to share the land with wolves, became much more abundant and one of the park's top predators. But the coyote's small size kept them from regulating the park's large ungulate populations, like wolves do. Though coyotes will kill elk calves, they prey mainly on pocket gophers, voles, and other small mammals. They also specialize in killing the fawns of pronghorn. The lack of carcasses left behind by wolves reduced the food normally available for foxes, badgers, raptors, coyotes and other scavengers.

So from 1995 to present, they reintroduced the wolves in that ecosystem. The elks, the primary prey of wolves in Yellowstone, have decreased in numbers within the park. Other factors such as drought, severe winters, and other large predators have also contributed to the decline in Yellowstone elk. But most importantly, as wolves returned, the behavior of elk changed; elk became more vigilant and were once again forced to stay on the move. Vulnerable along the rivers and streams, elk now spend more time in denser cover or on higher ground with better views for spotting predators. Consumption of vegetation by elk is thus restrained, giving many riparian areas a chance to finally recover. Aspens, willows, cottonwoods, and other vegetation have in many places resumed their natural growth.

When their favorite food and building material reappeared, beavers flourished, engineering broad wetlands that attract frogs, swans, and sandhill cranes. Stream banks, once picked clear of vegetation and eroded by hooves, erupted in wildflowers, which nourished insects, which in turn fed songbirds that nested among the thick willows. The water below now became shaded, deep, cool, and clear—a better habitat for aquatic-born insects and trout.

The coyotes' numbers dropped as they once again shared the land with wolves. Many coyotes were killed or driven away by wolves, helping to bring about a resurgence in pronghorn. A drop in coyotes leaves more gophers, and other rodents for foxes, raptors, and other mid-level carnivores to prey on.

The Wolves, now returned to their original habitat, play a vital role in keeping the world of predator and prey in balance. Once they've eaten their fill, the leftovers from their kills provide food for scavengers, including bald and golden eagles, magpies, coyotes, ravens, and bears. Another thing we have learned about the role of the Wolves is that they strengthen ungulates. Wolves eliminated sick, old and genetically inferior elk and deer, allowing the healthiest individuals to breed and perpetuate their species. They kill the coyotes, so rodent populations increase, benefiting struggling birds of prey. The Wolves also boost Ecotourism. The reintroduction of wolves to Yellowstone has attracted 150,000 new visitors each year, adding $35-million to the local economy annually.

What we can surmise is how the presence of Wolves plays a very important role in the ecosystems in which they live. Since 1995, when Wolves were reintroduced to the American West, research has shown that in many places they have helped revitalize and restore ecosystems. They improve habitat and increase populations of countless species from birds of prey to pronghorn, and even trout. The presence of wolves influences the population and behavior of their prey, changing the browsing and foraging patterns of prey animals and how they move about the land. This, in turn, ripples throughout plant and animal communities, often altering the landscape itself. For this reason Wolves are described as a "keystone species," whose presence is vital to maintaining the health, structure and balance of ecosystems.

The keystone species for the human race is the Woman. So what would happen if all women disappeared? How would the world change?

There would be an immediate impact on the workforce. Women comprise a large percentage in many countries, and their absence is felt acutely. Hospitals, schools, and businesses would have to adjust to cope with the loss of women employees. Though, the loss of women would not just be felt in the workforce. A world without women would be a very different place. From the food we eat to how our cities are designed, women are pivotal in shaping the world around us.

Today, being a woman means being strong enough to overcome adversity and discrimination; it means being secure in her identity, being able to speak her truth, supporting her family and community, and feeling unafraid to be both a feminist and feminine. Women are the backbone of families and communities. They provide care, support, and nurture to their families and are essential to the development of children. Women also play a significant role in community building and often take on leadership roles in community organizations.

Considering gender as a social construct can be fluid, as it exists on a continuum that can change over time. Someone's anatomy or biology has very little to do with their gender identity and is not what makes someone a woman. Being a woman means having a strong sense of identity, accepting your body as one that adapts and changes over time, being confident, and building up the people in your life.

While the roles of a woman are described as reproductive, productive and community-managing, women actually handle way more than that. For example, girls and women are generally expected to dress in typically feminine ways and be polite, accommodating, and nurturing. Men are generally expected to be strong, aggressive, and bold. Every society, ethnic group, and culture has gender role expectations, but they can be very different from group to group.

According to the most recent studies of this field, men find women more attractive when they are smart, intelligent, caring, confident, humorous, kind, independent, and supportive. Although these qualities may generally apply, what one man may find the most attractive may differ from another. Women are subject to so many expectations from themselves, their mates, their family, their kids and definitely society as a whole. That means what we need is to be equipped so we don't get overwhelmed by society. We need tools and skills to represent ourselves the best we should, primarily for ourselves and leading the way for the world. We are important, we matter, we are the keystone to humanity.

The next 10 chapters will highlight what we need in order to be successful in our mission on earth.

Knowledge is power!

CHAPTER 1: CONFIDENCE

Fake it till you make it!

What exactly does this expression mean? We've heard it from church, from family and friends, from inspirational quotes as well. How can someone fake until they make it? How do we know when we made it and it's no longer fake? How often do we have to do this? Does it work for every situation? Imagine if I want a baby, should I wear pregnancy clothes until I get pregnant? Or take my pregnancy vitamins until I get pregnant?

Well, luckily for me I will only be covering the confidence part of *fake it till you make it* because I sincerely have no idea about the pregnancy's predicament. To begin, let's define what confidence is and how it will apply into a woman's life but most importantly why it is important to display it.

Confidence is that feeling of self-assurance coming from your own appreciation of your abilities or qualities. Confidence is believing unconditionally in yourself, feeling comfortable about your true-self, knowing that you have an unlimited worth. The way this will apply in your life is by making people believe in you. Why is it important to earn the trust of society? Simply because a confident woman is attractive. This attractiveness will bring success, will help you to connect well with others and will lead to success at the end; to instantaneously create a flourishing woman.

Now let's work on how to achieve this level of confidence with all of the realities surrounding us. The past years have been extremely challenging for all of us. We had to face several battles, which we were never prepared for. We lost people we love the most, some of us don't have any emotional, physical or financial support. The actual odds of life make it so hard to even phantom the idea of confidence. While I totally understand because I am right here with you, I have been a Master of faking till I made it.

No matter what your religion is, if you even have one or not, we will use the concept of Faith toward our confidence building process. What is Faith? Faith is the assurance that the things we are believing in and expecting to see in reality will miraculously be formatted in real life. We are all dreaming to be happy, successful, satisfied and complete. We are not dreaming of these because it's where we are today but we are hoping.

A good example is when we go to work. We work before we get paid. Why? Because we are hoping that at the end of the week or the two weeks, we will have a check to compensate us for our past efforts. How do we know the company will not suddenly go out of business? How do we know our hours will be accounted for correctly? Of course we don't know! But we do faithfully go to work until we get to that payday and then we cash the check or call HR for missing hours.

Sadly it's so much easier for us to have confidence in others than in ourselves. Why is that? When we look at others we see exactly the image of themselves they displayed. Everyone wants to work for this big company, wants to go to this renowned university, wants to befriend this celebrity or partner with this successful business person. Why? Simply because they display confidence so we trust them to take us to where we are heading. Why can't we be that for others? What is holding us back? What are we afraid of? Who are we afraid to disappoint? Imagine if we had no fear. Now what are our qualities, skills, capacities? Everyone has all of the above in them and plenty. Often I've heard people telling me how lucky I was to know how to do hair or cook or talk or be extroverted. The truth is *"I fake it till I make it"*.

I remembered the first time I took a hair client, I was in Brussel. It was a family of 3 ladies who used to get their hair done prior with other stylists. I had only done my best friend Marcelle Kouassi's hair (may she R.I.P.) up to that point. We weren't very professional when I did my best friend's hair. We would play around, cook, shop, take a nap and take an entire day to do her hair. I didn't know how long I really took to do anyone's hair, making me wonder if I was capable of being still until I finished one client's hair? I didn't even know how much hair I needed, since we would just gather hair around the house. You may wonder how they found me and called me? I copied some big hair salon advertisements and dropped the post like I was even at that level. Well it kinda worked anyhow, I had the attention of a client and the fear of a mouse cornered by a cat. I went there, put on my big girl underwear and *faked it till I made it*. It was hard, draining, scary and stressful. I did it, though.

I was so happy and I ended up with a few referrals where I started my career as a professional braider.

My first big meal for a party of fifty was not from a last party of forty, nor was it from me cooking a meal for my family of four. Have I seen people cook big meals before? Yes I have. Was I the one cooking or helping? Nope. I took on the challenge with big fears in my stomach, uncertainty. What if I fail, what if I burn the food? Yet, it worked out surprisingly well. I still burn food in my kitchen from time to time, truth be told. Although, that day, I successfully cooked for several hours, crafting a meal to feed fifty people and it was good! What if I said no to this opportunity instead of *faking it till I made it*?

Confidence. It's an important tool in being a woman. Confidence. It's the first necessary step to get out there and become a successful woman. We are already phenomenal but how rewarding is it to be successful? Fears are what is blocking us to display confidence.

This is why Faith came into play. Focus on the outcome of what you want first and not how to get there. Now that you've already projected the result, then think of how to make it. So the *fake it* is just a projection of our goals but look at it as if we are living it. Our posture needs to show today, what it will look like tomorrow when we make it there. The same way we envision ourselves dressing up for our upcoming birthday or other events and we can see the look we will portray, it's how we need to work on confidence. We have to lead the way into our lives for others to follow. How do we want others to have confidence in us if we don't have it for ourselves?

The right steps to take in order to accomplish a healthy level of confidence is to write down:

1- Our Goals
2- Our Skills
3- Our Values
4- Our Fears
5- Our Obstacles
6- Our Assets
7- Our Time Frame

8- Always, always remember to put a date on our paper.

A date is so important! A date is telling you that it's official! You are now in business!

CHAPTER 2: PERSONALITY

I like her, I totally trust her, she is amazing!

Having a great personality is wholly beneficial to live in society. From Wikipedia, Personality is the characteristic sets of behaviors, cognitions, and emotional patterns that are formed from biological and environmental factors, and which change over time.

There are three criteria that characterize personality traits:

1- Consistency
2- Stability
3- Individual Differences

To have a personality trait, individuals must be somewhat consistent across situations in their behaviors related to the trait. How is that in order to be consistent, you have to be consistent? Well the answer is simple, consistency is consistency.

There's no other way to be identified with a consistent personality if we don't display its consistent behavior. Why is it beneficial for our personality to be consistent? Others will know what to expect from us. That expectation brings peace in mind. Doesn't matter if you end up saying yes or saying no, people will know where to stand with you if you're consistent and this is a crucial character trait to have.

As a woman, it's important to have a defined personality so we don't fall into the bipolar section, in which society is so pressured to add folks into. May your Yes be Yes and your No be No. As women we have to show stability in our behavior to reassure our surroundings. How many times do we naturally avoid unstable people? They are scarier than a good Halloween costume.

Why is being stable relevant or important should we ask? Living and spending time in a loving, secure and stable environment is incredibly important for all of us. We all want to feel like we belong, that we are loved and cared for. Imagine how disturbing it is to deal with an unstable individual… we certainly don't want to be one of those.

We want to inspire Trust, Love, Loyalty and Consistency in those qualities. We are able to maintain a steady and healthy circle of relationships. Our personal stamp is our personality. What we are made of, our components!

In the long run this particular trait will help us select our options and determine our destiny. Knowing ourselves is primordial for the rest of our lives. Life is based on choices to make in order to keep advancing to the next challenge. Knowing who we are, what we can or cannot handle is a key to making the right choice moving forward. I know who I want or not want to be around, who to keep or not keep around me.

Your personality guides your behaviors and habits, and both play a big part in your overall health. The way you handle stress, your activity level, how often you socialize or see your doctor — all of these things are affected by your personality traits, starting early on.

How do others impact us?

This goes both ways, and people learn to interact with us based on our personality. When we behave differently than our normal set of personality traits, people may or may not take time to adjust to the situation.

Personality also affects our ability to interact with others, which can impact our career success. For example, individuals who become more agreeable, kind and compassionate, also tend to place more emphasis on social and family/relationship goals over time. On the other hand, individuals who become more responsible, organized and self-controlled tend to value more economic and family goals.

Therefore personality development and success always go hand in hand. Personality development is the preparation for a person to achieve their goals in life. This will also help you not only to build a better relationship with yourself but with those around you.

The most important action to take is to be someone who is consistent, always behaves in the same way, has the same attitudes towards people or things, or achieves the same level of success in something.

Patience is the key to consistency. We have to be patient and focus our efforts diligently in one direction in order to produce quality, lasting, tangible results. Consistency is key when it comes to building trust and credibility within our community. When establishing a brand image of ourselves that is cohesive across all areas, you show our professionalism, devotion, reliability, and commitment to our promises. Ants act as an excellent example of consistency. They keep moving consistently to find food. They keep at their tasks until they find their food. The same goes with honey bees. Their job is doing consistent work for the honey making process.

Establishing our personality also implies that we show stability. Stable people tend to have long, satisfying relationships. They do well in their jobs.

Their lives are relatively free from unnecessary drama. They make good decisions regarding their health and finances. Stability makes you able to withstand difficult situations, handle adversity, and remain productive and capable throughout any challenges that you may encounter. A woman displaying a stable personality, will show calm and reasonableness in most situations. Also, their mood does not change suddenly. Human beings yearn for predictability and stability. We don't function well in unstable conditions, or more accurately, we don't think we function well in unstable conditions. While we can accommodate ourselves within challenges, we ultimately prefer not to. We understand that we are quasi different from each other and those differences can be appreciated, especially when complementary to each other.

An important area to master in order to build a very trustworthy personality is to be able to identify and understand personal values and beliefs. Therefore, a woman should follow certain steps:

- Self-Reflection: Take some time to introspect and reflect on your thoughts, feelings, and actions. Ask yourself questions such as, "What is important to me?", "What do I truly believe in?", and "What are my core values?"

- Identify Core Values: Based on your self-reflection, identify the values that are most important to you. These can be honesty, compassion, integrity, fairness, respect, courage, etc. Make a list of these core values and prioritize them according to their significance in your life.

- Evaluate Beliefs: Examine your beliefs and question their origins and validity. Reflect on whether these beliefs align with your core values and if they contribute positively to your personal growth and well-being. Be open to challenging and updating beliefs that no longer serve you.

- Seek Diverse Perspectives: Engage in conver-sations with people from different backgrounds and cultures to gain a broader understanding of different values and beliefs. This exposure will help you expand your horizons and develop a more inclusive and empathetic mindset.

- Stay True to Yourself: Remain authentic and true to your own values and beliefs, even in challenging situations. Be mindful of peer pressure or societal expectations that may sway you away from your personal convictions. Trusting and following your own moral compass will strengthen your character and build trust with others.

- Practice Self-Awareness: Continuously observe your thoughts, actions, and behaviors to ensure they align with your identified values and beliefs. Regularly self-reflect and make adjustments if necessary, striving for consistency in your words and actions.

- Lead by Example: Live your life in a way that showcases your values and beliefs. This will inspire others and attract like-minded individuals who appreciate your authenticity and integrity. By being a role model, you can positively influence and motivate others to build their own strong and trustworthy personalities.

Remember, building a strong and trustworthy personality is an ongoing process. It requires self-reflection, continuous learning, and consistent practice. Embrace personal growth, embrace diversity, and always strive to be the best version of yourself.

Another important area, second but not least important skill, is to obtain emotional intelligence and empathy. This primarily is to develop self-confidence and assertiveness skills.

To develop self-confidence and assertiveness skills, a woman can focus on various aspects of her personality and behavior. Here are some steps to accomplish this:

- Identify Strengths and Weaknesses: Start by reflecting on personal strengths and weaknesses. Recognize the areas where you feel confident and the ones where you may lack assertiveness. This self-awareness will provide a foundation for growth.

- Set Realistic Goals: Determine specific goals that will help you become more self-confident and assertive. These goals can be small, achievable steps that gradually build your confidence. For example, setting a goal to express your opinion in a meeting or assertively asking for what you need.

- Enhance Self-Belief: Cultivate a positive mindset and belief in yourself. Challenge negative self-talk and replace it with positive affirmations. Remind yourself of past achievements and successes to reinforce your belief in your abilities.

- Increase Self-Care: Taking care of yourself physically, emotionally, and mentally is crucial. Engage in activities that bring you joy, practice self-compassion, and prioritize self-care. When you feel good about yourself, it's easier to exude confidence and assertiveness.

- Practice Assertive Communication: Develop effective communication skills by learning to express your thoughts, needs, and boundaries clearly and respectfully. Practice using "I" statements to convey your feelings and opinions without being aggressive or passive.

- Embrace Challenges: Step out of your comfort zone and embrace new challenges. By facing and overcoming obstacles, you will build resilience and strengthen your sense of self. Remember that failures and setbacks are opportunities for growth, not reflections of your worth.

- Seek Support: Surround yourself with positive and supportive people who believe in your abilities. Share your goals and aspirations with trusted friends or mentors who can provide guidance and encouragement along the way.

- Continuous Learning: Take advantage of opportunities for personal and professional development to further enhance your self-confidence and assertiveness. Attend workshops, read books, or enroll in courses that focus on building these skills.

By following these steps, a woman can gradually develop a strong and trustworthy personality, characterized by self-confidence and assertiveness.

Remember again, and I will keep reminding you, building these traits is a lifelong journey, so be patient and kind to yourself throughout the process.

Another great skill in addition is to practice good communication and listening. To build a strong and trustworthy personality, practicing good communication and listening skills is crucial. Effective communication is not only about expressing oneself but also about actively listening to others.

Let me list some steps you can take to improve your communication and listening skills:

- Pay Attention: When engaging in a conversation, give your undivided attention to the speaker. Maintain eye contact and avoid distractions such as checking your phone or looking around the room.

- Be Present: Stay in the moment and focus on the conversation at hand. Avoid interrupting or thinking about what you will say next while the other person is speaking. Truly listening shows respect and helps you understand the speaker's perspective.

- Show Empathy: Try to understand the speaker's emotions and perspective. Put yourself in their shoes and respond accordingly. Demonstrating empathy helps build trust and strengthens relationships.

- Ask Open-Ended Questions: Encourage the speaker to elaborate on their thoughts and feelings by asking open-ended questions. This shows your interest and allows for deeper conversations.

- Practice Active Listening: Engage in active listening by nodding, using verbal cues like "I see," "I understand," or "Tell me more." This shows that you are actively engaged in the conversation and encourages the speaker to continue sharing their thoughts.

- Reflect on Your Own Communication Style: Take time to reflect on how you communicate with others. Are there any patterns or behaviors that you can improve upon? Self-awareness is key to personal growth and developing a trustworthy personality.

- Seek Feedback: Ask trusted friends, family members, or colleagues for feedback on your communication skills. Their insights can provide valuable perspectives and help identify areas for improvement.

Once again building a trustworthy personality takes time and consistent effort. Practice makes perfect so keep applying good communication and listening skills. You can then establish meaningful connections, build trust, and become a more reliable and trustworthy woman.

The environment matters a lot when you are in the process of creating a powerful YOU. Build a strong support system and surround yourself with positive influences. Firstly, it is essential to identify the people in your life who bring positivity, encouragement, and support. These individuals can be family members, close friends, mentors, or even colleagues who inspire and motivate you. Surrounding yourself with such people will create an environment that fosters personal growth and helps in building a trustworthy personality.

To build a strong support system, actively seek out individuals who share similar values, goals, and aspirations. Engage in activities or join communities where you can connect with like-minded individuals. This could be through participating in sports, volunteering for a cause, attending workshops or seminars, or joining social or professional groups. By doing so, you increase the chances of meeting people who can provide the necessary support and influence you positively.

Additionally, it is important to evaluate your existing relationships and assess whether they contribute positively to your personal development. If you find that certain relationships are toxic, draining, or constantly bring negativity into your life, it may be necessary to distance yourself from those individuals. Surrounding yourself with positive influences means surrounding yourself with people who uplift and support you, rather than hinder your growth.

Moreover, in order to strengthen your support system, it is crucial to be an active participant within these relationships. Show genuine care and interest in the lives of your support network. Be available to lend a listening ear, offer advice or assistance, and celebrate their successes. By being a reliable source of support for others, you will inherently attract individuals who reciprocate that support to you, creating a stronger and more trustworthy network.

In conclusion, building a strong support system and surrounding yourself with positive influences is a vital step in developing a trustworthy personality. By connecting with like-minded individuals, distancing yourself from negative relationships, and actively participating in supportive relationships, you are paving the way for personal growth, self-improvement, and trustworthiness.

I mentioned earlier the importance of developing emotional intelligence and empathy skills. In order to develop these things, a woman can follow several steps:

- Self-Awareness: Start by becoming more aware of your own emotions, thoughts, and behaviors. Take time to reflect on your feelings and understand why you react in certain ways. This will help you gain a deeper understanding of yourself and how your emotions influence your actions.

- Active Listening: Practice active listening skills to better understand the emotions and perspectives of others. When engaging in conversations, focus on the speaker, maintain eye contact, and avoid interrupting. Show genuine interest and empathy by asking questions and reflecting back on what they've said.

- Empathy Cultivation: Put yourself in someone else's shoes and try to understand their experiences and feelings. Practice empathy by imagining how you would feel or react in a similar situation. This will help you develop a more compassionate and understanding approach towards others.

- Emotional Regulation: Learn to manage and regulate your own emotions effectively. When faced with challenging situations, take a moment to pause and reflect before responding. Identify your triggers and develop coping mechanisms, such as deep breathing or journaling, to help control emotional reactions and maintain a calm demeanor.

- Non-Verbal Communication: Pay attention to non-verbal cues such as facial expressions, body language, and tone of voice. Being aware of these subtle signals can help you understand the emotions behind someone's words and respond accordingly. Additionally, practice conveying your own emotions through non-verbal means to enhance your communication skills.

- Empathetic Communication: Practice expressing empathy in your interactions. Acknowledge and validate others' emotions by using phrases like "I understand how you feel" or "That must be really difficult for you." This will help build trust and establish strong connections with others.

- Seek Diverse Perspectives: Surround yourself with diverse individuals and actively seek out different perspectives. Engaging with people from various backgrounds and cultures will broaden your understanding of emotions and help you develop a more inclusive and empathetic mindset.

- Practice Emotional Intelligence in Daily Life: Apply your emotional intelligence and empathy skills in various situations, both personal and professional. Whether it's supporting a friend through a tough time or collaborating with colleagues, consciously utilize your newfound abilities to build trust and foster positive relationships.

By consistently practicing these steps, a woman can develop emotional intelligence and empathy skills, thereby building a strong and trustworthy personality. You will encounter a lot of bumps on the road, but stay focused on the GOAL!

CHAPTER 3: PLAN

Why is it important for a woman to establish a plan in her life?

It is important for a woman to establish a plan in her life to set a clear direction and purpose for herself. By having a plan, as a woman you can have a sense of control over your life and work towards achieving your goals and aspirations. We start by identifying personal goals and aspirations as a crucial step in establishing a plan. It allows a woman to have a clear understanding of what she wants to achieve and what is important to her. Personal goals can vary widely depending on individual preferences, values, and life circumstances and that we understand.

Therefore in order to complete this sub-task, I will share a list of personal goals and aspirations that a woman may and should consider:

- Career Goals: These may include achieving a certain position or level of success in her chosen profession, starting her own business, or pursuing further education or training to enhance her skills.

- Relationship Goals: These may include finding a life partner, building a healthy and fulfilling relationship, or starting a family.

- Personal Development Goals: These may include improving self-confidence, cultivating a positive mindset, enhancing communication skills, or learning new hobbies or interests.

- Financial Goals: These may include saving for retirement, buying a house, starting investments, or achieving financial independence.

- Health and Fitness Goals: These may include maintaining a healthy lifestyle, setting fitness targets, participating in regular physical activities, or adopting a balanced diet.

- Travel and Adventure Goals: These may include exploring new places, experiencing different cultures, embarking on adventurous activities, or crossing off destinations from a bucket list.

- Contribution Goals: These may include volunteering for a cause, supporting charitable organizations, or making a positive impact in the community.

It is important to note that personal goals can evolve over time and may require adjustments as circumstances change. A woman may prioritize certain goals over others based on her current life stage, resources, and personal values. Regularly reviewing and revisiting these goals is essential to ensure they align with her overall plan and aspirations.

In conclusion, by identifying personal goals and aspirations, a woman can establish a plan that provides direction and purpose in her life. This plan allows her to work towards achieving her goals, experience personal growth, and lead a fulfilling and meaningful life.

I believe you'd want to know where to start. First evaluate your current circumstances and identify areas for improvement. It is important for a woman to establish a plan in her life in order to gain clarity, focus, and direction towards achieving her goals and aspirations. By creating a plan, she can carefully evaluate her current circumstances, identify areas for improvement, and ultimately work towards a more fulfilling and successful life. To evaluate her current circumstances, a woman can start by conducting a thorough self-assessment. This involves introspection and reflection on various aspects of her life, such as her career, relationships, health, and personal growth. She should analyze her strengths, weaknesses, opportunities, and threats in each area, taking into account her skills, passions, and values. By understanding her current situation, she can identify any gaps or areas that require improvement.

Once your evaluation is complete, the next step is to identify the areas for improvement. This can be done by setting specific and measurable goals in different aspects of your life. For example, if you want to advance in your career, you could set a goal to acquire new skills or pursue further education. If you want to improve your health and well-being, you could set a few goals related to exercise, nutrition, or stress management.

When identifying areas for improvement, it is essential to prioritize based on what is most important and achievable given the current circumstances. A woman should consider her resources, time availability, and any potential obstacles that may arise. It is important to set realistic and attainable goals to maintain motivation and ensure progress. Additionally, it can be helpful to seek feedback from trusted individuals such as mentors, friends, or family members. They can provide valuable insights and perspectives on areas that may not be apparent to the woman herself. This feedback can further guide her in identifying areas for improvement and refining her plan.

You can see why it is important to surrender ourselves to insights of valuable individuals.

To conclude this small segment, by evaluating current circumstances and identifying areas for improvement, a woman can establish a well-rounded plan for her life. This plan will provide you with a roadmap to navigate challenges and make informed decisions that align with your goals and aspirations. By continuously reassessing and adjusting your plan as needed, you can ensure personal growth, fulfillment, and success in various aspects of your life.

As a woman, it is important to establish a plan in your life in order to have a sense of direction, focus, and control over your future. Creating a plan with specific actions and timelines to achieve your goals is crucial for several reasons:

- Clarity of Goals: By establishing a plan, you can clearly define your goals and aspirations. This allows you to have a clear vision of what you want to achieve and helps you stay motivated and focused.

- Prioritization: A well-developed plan helps you prioritize your goals and actions. It enables you to identify what needs to be done first and what can be tackled later. By setting priorities, you can allocate your time, energy, and resources efficiently, ensuring that you make progress towards your goals.

- Accountability: Having a plan with specific actions and timelines allows you to hold yourself accountable. It provides a framework for tracking your progress and evaluating whether you are on track or need to make adjustments. This accountability keeps you committed and disciplined towards achieving your goals.

- Overcoming Obstacles: Life is full of challenges and obstacles that can deter you from achieving your goals. However, with a well-established plan, you can anticipate potential hurdles and develop strategies to overcome them. By identifying obstacles in advance, you can be better prepared to handle them and stay focused on your path to success.

- Time Management: A plan with specific timelines helps you manage your time effectively. By breaking down your goals into actionable steps with deadlines, you can allocate your time wisely and avoid procrastination. This ensures that you make steady progress towards your goals and avoid unnecessary delays.

- Personal Growth: Establishing a plan in your life allows for personal growth and self-improvement. It pushes you outside your comfort zone, encourages you to set challenging goals, and motivates you to learn new skills. By continuously working towards your plan, you can develop new strengths, gain confidence, and evolve into the best version of yourself.

It is important for a woman to establish a plan in her life. By creating a plan with specific actions and timelines to achieve her goals, she gains clarity, prioritizes effectively, holds herself accountable, overcomes obstacles, manages time efficiently, and experiences personal growth. This empowers her to take control of her life, achieve her aspirations, and live a fulfilling and successful life.

While all of this is achievable, the most important and bottom-line action to take is to regularly review and adjust the plan as necessary. A plan will need adjustment based on certain milestones reached or circumstances occurring during the process. I was able to understand early on that as a woman, it is important to establish a plan in my life for several reasons.

Firstly, having a plan provides a sense of direction and purpose. It allows me to set clear goals and work towards achieving them. Without a plan, it becomes easy to feel lost or overwhelmed with the uncertainties and challenges that life presents. Secondly, having a plan helps in prioritizing tasks and making informed decisions. By outlining my objectives and breaking them down into smaller, manageable steps, I can focus my energy and resources on what truly matters. This enhances efficiency and productivity in both personal and professional aspects of life.

Furthermore, a well-thought-out plan enables me to anticipate and prepare for potential obstacles or setbacks. It allows me to have contingency measures in place and adapt to changing circumstances.

It is important for a woman to establish a plan in her life in order to have a sense of direction and purpose. We are in agreement with this fact by now.

Here is a detailed idea to the reviewing process that I think will clarify further.

Regularly reviewing and adjusting the plan is crucial to ensure it remains aligned with current circumstances and goals. Life is dynamic, and situations change over time. By reviewing the plan periodically, a woman can assess whether her goals and priorities have shifted or if external factors have influenced her circumstances.

To begin with, it is important to schedule regular review sessions to evaluate the progress made towards the goals outlined in the plan. This can be done monthly, quarterly, or annually, depending on the individual's preference and the complexity of the plan.

During these review sessions, the woman should reflect on her accomplishments, identify any challenges faced, and assess the overall effectiveness of her approach. During the review process, it is vital to consider the current circumstances and any changes that may have occurred. For example, if the woman's financial situation has changed significantly, she may need to adjust her plan to accommodate new financial goals or reevaluate her savings and investment strategies. Similarly, if her personal or professional priorities have shifted, she may need to make modifications to the plan to align with these changes.

Additionally, it is important to assess whether the goals set in the plan are realistic and achievable. If circumstances have significantly changed and certain goals are no longer feasible, it may be necessary to revise or replace them with new objectives that are more attainable. Reasoning behind these decisions stems from the understanding that life is constantly evolving, and it is essential to adapt accordingly.

By regularly reviewing and adjusting the plan, a woman can ensure that she remains on track and continues to progress towards her desired outcomes. It allows her to stay flexible and responsive to changing circumstances, ultimately increasing her chances of success and fulfillment in various aspects of her life.

In summary, this proactive approach empowers her to make necessary adjustments and stay focused on her journey towards personal and professional fulfillment. Regularly review and adjust the plan as necessary to ensure it remains aligned with current circumstances and goals.

This may sound like a repetition but trust me it's that serious. You should understand what a **Plan** is by definition, which is an intention or decision about what one is going to do. Just that simple, intention or decision. An intention is what we aim for.

So what are you aiming for in life? What is your target? How do you personally identify your target? What are your dreams? Are you dreaming or aren't you? What's holding you from aiming? If you are aiming, how far are you aiming? Are you satisfied with your goals?

Starting a plan is everything. The most important thing is to START.

- Define what your final goal is.
- Write down the steps to get there.
- Prioritize your to-do list.
- Add a deadline.
- Set milestones.
- What are your assets?
- Have a vision of your plan of action.
- Monitor.

- Evaluate.
- Update your plan with any achievements or modifications.

Let's pretend Sophie's goal is to be financially independent so she plans it.

Plan is Financially independent

- Steps: Get a job, a side hustle, complete my education or find a rich husband.

Questions:

Is your actual job the answer, if you have one? Is it enough income for your daily needs? Do you have a job? What are your other streams of income? Yes, because you may need more than one way to bring money in and we will delve more into this part in the chapter on finances.

- Prioritize your steps.

If it's a job, make sure you are doing the most you can. Are you in a leadership position? Did you negotiate the highest pay possible? Is your side hustle on your daily schedule? How many hours a day do you devote to this business? Is it school? Are you turning in your assignments? Taking double classes? Did you choose the correct educational needs in relation to your plan? Or have you found a rich husband? Where are you hanging out? Who are your friends circle? Every step that you take needs to be carefully assessed. Those steps need to be realistic while your plan may be unrealistic.

It's important to write steps that you can follow with minimum efforts and then cultivate into a maximum effort. Nothing comes easy!

- The deadline!

Yes, you need a deadline, as opposed to your entire life to achieve the goal. When do you want to become financially independent? In a year or in 5 years? Based on your time frame, you will be able to set your milestones and celebrate every one of them.

Yes it's important to celebrate our milestones. It gives us a sense of success and achievements. Some women believe that financial stability is what is needed for them to feel accomplished; others believe accumulating diplomas will be all they need.

The most important thing is to write it down!

Next is to define the steps. We will cover financial possibilities in the next chapter but if it's you, make sure to understand how far you want to go before you settle as a wealthy woman. When it comes to diplomas, make sure it's something you are passionate about. The main reason is that it's not cheap to complete your education.

Don't only focus on the income from your job. While a job may post a high salary, it takes a lot of disappointment before you actually receive the check.

Depending on your status, a lot of taxes may pile up and fees as well as the realization to pay back the student loans turns up. Once you figure out what you want to do and make your list, commit to it. Very, very, very important to prioritize your lists. The way to go about it really depends on what you want to achieve.

Short-term tasks and easy tasks should be achieved first and celebrate each time they are reached. Then use the momentum and keep checking off items off your lists.

Remember to impose yourself on a deadline and work your hardest to reach it. Make sure to visualize the result of your plan. It makes it real and feels more accessible. Celebrate, celebrate and celebrate any little, tiny milestones and stay focused!

CHAPTER 4: FINANCES

A stable financial situation is crucial for women, as it has been found that narrowing the gender gap in the banking system would promote greater stability and enhance economic growth.

Studies conducted by the International Monetary Fund (IMF) have highlighted the benefits of greater inclusion of women in various roles within the financial sector, such as users, providers, and regulators of financial services. Moreover, research conducted by the Financial Health Network has consistently shown a significant gap in the financial health of men and women, indicating the pressing need for improvements in women's financial situations.

What are the simple fundamentals of finance you may ask? Well for starters, finance is defined as the management of money to include activities such as investing, borrowing, lending, budgeting, saving, and forecasting. Why is it important for a woman to be in charge of her finances? Case studies have also provided insights into the importance of financial stability for women. A recent study conducted by Bank of America revealed that 94% of women believe that they will be personally responsible for their financial wellness. This finding emphasizes the understanding among women of their own financial circumstances and the need for a stable financial situation. Additionally, an analysis conducted by researchers has shown that women with higher financial self-efficacy, meaning greater confidence in managing their finances, tend to have better financial management outcomes.

Overall, the statistics and case studies mentioned above support the findings that a stable financial situation is of paramount importance for women. Closing the gender gap in the banking system and promoting greater inclusion of women in financial services can lead to improved economic growth and financial well-being for women.

What are the issues that women encounter the most when it comes to finances? Financial stability is undeniably crucial for women as it has a significant impact on their overall well-being. Having a stable financial situation not only provides a sense of security but also enables women to have control over their lives and make decisions independently.

One key aspect of financial stability is economic empowerment. When women are financially stable, they are better equipped to support themselves and their families. They have the means to meet their basic needs such as food, shelter, healthcare, and education. This, in turn, leads to an improved quality of life and overall well-being for both themselves and their loved ones. Furthermore, financial stability plays a vital role in women's mental and emotional well-being. When women have a stable financial situation, they experience reduced stress and anxiety related to financial insecurity. They are more likely to feel empowered and confident in their abilities to manage their finances effectively. This sense of control and confidence positively impacts their mental health, leading to increased overall well-being.

Will great financing be a determination in the affirmation of a successful woman? Is great financing what people call *'what do you bring on the table'* perhaps? Financial stability also opens up opportunities for personal and professional growth. With a stable financial situation, women can invest in their education, skill development, and career advancement. They have the flexibility to pursue their passions, start their own businesses, or take on leadership roles. This not only enhances their self-esteem and self-worth but also contributes to their overall happiness and fulfillment.

Additionally, financial stability plays a crucial role in women's physical well-being. It enables them to afford proper healthcare services, preventive screenings, and necessary medications. They are less likely to delay or neglect their health needs due to financial constraints. As a result, they can maintain good health, prevent illnesses, and address any health concerns promptly, leading to a higher level of physical well-being.

Based on the findings, it is evident that a stable financial situation holds immense importance for women. It acts as a catalyst for their empowerment, economic independence, and overall well-being. To ensure the achievement of gender equality and the advancement of women's rights, it is crucial to promote financial literacy, provide access to financial resources, and create an enabling environment that supports women's economic growth and stability. How can a woman be financially secure?

Those questions are going to be answered in this chapter with much details and directions to follow.

What we need to retain is that a woman in charge of her finances is able to make informed decisions concerning the management of her assets. She is also in position to set the proper financial goals, and make smart investments in alignment with her values. As women we need to control our finances to access the tools that will help us make financial decisions independently. Owning your money is important because this will give you an input in the world's decisions.

Whenever we start managing our finances, we achieve a better perspective on where and how we can invest or spend our money. This can help us work on a budget or create savings. Begin saving, creating emergency funds, and building credit are just a few important steps. Being able to set aside a specified amount for savings when creating a monthly budget should be a priority.

It's important to notice that Financial stability is a crucial factor in a healthy relationship and having a stable source of income can provide peace of mind and security. Being employed can also indicate a strong work ethic and responsibility, which are important qualities in a partner. So what you bring on a table could be halfway fulfilled by being in control of our finances.

While Financial stability can mean different things to different people, in this case it means you can pay your bills comfortably, you're on track with your money-related goals, you have little to no debt, and you can live the life you want. For us women, growing money is more important than saving money for sustainable growth. We are born to multiply everything we ever receive. Remember the saying: you give a woman a spermatozoid she gives you a baby, you give her a house she makes it a home.

A woman needs to become a finance manager or hire one. We need to allocate funds into profitable ventures or make investments that give reasonable returns with safety on the investment made.

Five major things every woman should know about their finances:

- Your credit report and score matter.
- Know your exact total debt amount.
- Account for all of your income sources.
- Get a big picture of your spending.
- Make sure you access and track all accounts.

Tracking your spending is actually the key to dramatically improving your finances.

It's also imperative to create a realistic monthly budget and to honor it. Build up your savings one penny at the time even if it feels like it takes forever. Pay your bills on time every month, start with one bill and add a new bill on time each month. Cut back on recurring charges, finding a way to make them disappear. For every big purchase, save up cash to afford them. Consult a financial advisor and get on a plan. Create more than one stream of income. We will go into details on these matters in chapter 6.

Respecting and applying these ideas can lead to greater financial confidence and a more positive outlook on life.

CHAPTER 5: WARDROBE

Embarking on a new goal; what role a proper wardrobe plays in a woman's life.

A proper wardrobe plays a significant role in a woman's life as it offers various benefits and has an impact on her overall well-being and confidence. One of the advantages is that it allows a woman to focus more on quality rather than quantity when it comes to her clothing choices. By having a well-curated wardrobe consisting of classic pieces and trendy statement items, she can effortlessly create stylish and elegant outfits suitable for any occasion.

Furthermore, dressing well is considered the cornerstone of having great taste and is essential in establishing a classy and elegant wardrobe. A woman's wardrobe reflects her personal style and can leave a lasting impression on others. It not only enhances her appearance but also showcases her attention to detail and refined sense of fashion.

Clothes can hold a significant emotional significance, and this is why it is important to ensure that the clothes in a woman's closet do not hold negative emotions or guilt. A well-organized and clutter-free wardrobe can contribute to a woman's overall emotional well-being and help her feel more positive and confident. It allows her to let go of any negative associations and choose to wear clothes that make her feel good about herself.

Having a proper wardrobe can also have a positive impact on a woman's daily life and energy levels. Instead of feeling overwhelmed by an excessive amount of clothing options, a well-crafted wardrobe enables her to make decisions more quickly and efficiently when shopping. This saves time and reduces decision fatigue, allowing her to focus her energy on other aspects of her life.

Lastly, dressing well can have a significant effect on a woman's self-esteem and motivation. When a woman feels good about her appearance, it boosts her confidence and positively influences her mindset for the day. Even during challenging times, dressing well can help uplift her mood and provide the motivation to face the day with a positive attitude.

- Boosts Confidence: Wearing well-fitted and stylish clothing that suits your body type and personality can significantly enhance a woman's self-confidence. When you feel good about how you look, it positively impacts your overall self-esteem and demeanor.

- Professional Image: A proper wardrobe is essential for professional settings. Dressing appropriately and maintaining a polished appearance can help women make a positive impression in the workplace. It can also enhance their credibility, professionalism, and chances of career advancement.

- Personal Expression: Clothing is a form of self-expression and allows women to showcase their individuality and personal style. A well-curated wardrobe offers a range of options to express oneself through fashion choices, reflecting their unique personality and creativity.

- Versatility and Adaptability: A proper wardrobe consists of versatile and timeless pieces that can be mixed and matched to create various outfits for different occasions. Investing in quality essentials such as a little black dress, tailored blazers, or classic denim allows women to effortlessly transition from casual to formal or from day to night.

- Time and Money Savings: Having a well-thought-out wardrobe eliminates the need for impulsive shopping or constantly buying new clothes. When you have a selection of key pieces that you love and that suit you well, it becomes easier to create outfits and reduces the time spent on deciding what to wear. It also saves money in the long run by avoiding unnecessary purchases.

- Improved Organization: A proper wardrobe encourages organization and helps women keep their clothing, accessories, and shoes in order. With a systematic approach to arranging their wardrobe, women can easily locate items, avoid clutter, and maintain the longevity of their clothes.

- Positive Body Image: A proper wardrobe embraces and celebrates diverse body types, allowing women to feel comfortable and confident in their own skin. Having clothing that fits well and flatters their unique physique promotes a positive body image and encourages self-acceptance.

A proper wardrobe goes beyond the mere act of dressing up. It plays a vital role in a woman's life by boosting confidence, enhancing professional image, allowing personal expression, providing versatility, saving time and money, improving organization, and promoting a positive body image. By recognizing the benefits of a well-curated wardrobe, women can harness its power to positively impact various aspects of their lives.

Every woman wants and deserves to look nice and dress well. Not only because it would present her in a good light in a social setting, but also because it is fulfilling, mood-boosting and imperative for self-esteem like we already discovered. It reflects a good character. Dressing well and staying well-groomed conveys more than just power, authority, and confidence. It shows that you have self-respect. The way you decide to present yourself to the world is how they'll take you.

A classy woman is someone who exudes sophistication and poise. She knows how to dress impeccably, is always well-groomed, is classy in her demeanor, speaks with confidence, and radiates self-respect. A classy woman leaves an impression - she's unforgettable. How do we define someone who is well-dressed? She is wearing fashionable or elegant clothes. She's always well-dressed. Automatically, society assumes that she is smart, intelligent, elegant, stylish and chic.

Clothes Can Make You Feel Powerful. High-quality, well-tailored clothing can help you feel more confident and powerful, allowing you to take on challenges at work and in your personal life. Research has shown that wearing formal clothing can change the way you view and approach situations actually. The clothing you wear has a direct impact on what people assume about who and what you are. The better you are dressed, the more respect and positive attention you are going to earn.

So the next question is: what is qualified to be well-dressed?

- Wear well-fitting clothes always, unless of course it's intentionally a part of the fashion.
- Choose the right colors, nothing too flashy.
- Add elegant layers, color coordinate or match fabrics.
- Show off your best features.
- Don't over complicate your outfits, the simplest the better.
- Wear classic and timeless pieces so no matter what's in fashion or if you need to stay on budget, you are always good.
- Stay away from trends because trends are not for leaders. Plus, create your own based on your personality.
- Know your fashion style.

How many items should a wardrobe have, women often asked or wondered? The researchers found that a "sufficient" wardrobe consists of 74 garments and 20 outfits in total. As an example, they've suggested six outfits for work, three outfits for home wear, three outfits for sports, two outfits for festive occasions, plus four outdoor jackets and trousers or skirts.

Personally I am a sucker for a good trench, a basic white shirt, a basic cotton Tee, a black blazer, dark blue denim, a cashmere sweater, white trainers, black heels, black flats as my base then I add other items I see fit.

Buying new clothes is now cheaper, faster, and easier than ever before. But it's not a good idea to renew your wardrobe every week. Under normal wear and tear, the average life expectancy of clothing could be more than 2 years. So while a great classy wardrobe is a must, no need to break the bank for it.

CHAPTER 6: JOB & A BUSINESS

We mentioned earlier the importance of having multiple streams of income.

How many income streams is good for a woman? It depends on the lifestyle you want and the skills you have. But 65% of millionaires have at least three streams of income, and that's an achievable number for most people. Personally my goal was to have ten streams of income and I was able to reach my goal over the course of a few years. The easiest and most reliable way to add more income is by investing but you need capital.

If you're new to this, having multiple streams of income just means that you have income from several different sources. For example, if you have your normal 9-5 job and an Ebay store that you manage, then you have two different ways of making money; therefore, you have multiple streams of income.

The first thing to keep in mind is to always have a job because it provides the ultimate financial security. A job can provide you with a steady income, which can help you cover living expenses and save money for the future. Nevertheless, a good health insurance, a sense of purpose, a retirement plan, some set of skills, definitely valuable connections which can be beneficial down the road, and some of them let you enjoy discounts and perks.

On the other hand, becoming an entrepreneur presents his benefits as well as a secondary source of income. The definition of being an entrepreneur is being a person who starts a business while taking on all the financial risks associated with starting a business. You still could do all that while working a regular 9-5 job. Entrepreneurship doesn't bestow or imply any moral or ethical benefits. Having a business isn't necessarily a better way of living, it's just another way of living.

This is your life. Any decision that you make for yourself will be correct -- as long as you're honest about how you want to live and the goals you want to achieve. Running a business while working full-time can be extremely time-consuming. However, every employee owes their employer their full attention during work hours, so you should work on your side business only during your free time. Refrain from running your own company during work hours for your job. It's ethical to keep them separate, plus it sets a better base for your own business.

Can you run a business and work full-time?

This is a question that has been asked so many times. Yes, I did work 2 full time jobs and run a business. So it is possible to work full time and start a business, but it requires sticking to a schedule and being disciplined. I had to miss a lot of parties, fun and friends. A lot of my personal birthdays were not celebrated. The best schedule I had was to start working on my business venture a few hours before and/or after working at my jobs each day and try to dedicate all of my weekends.

It is definitely a myth to think that entrepreneurs are born, the reality is that entrepreneurs are made by being committed to calculated risk taking and perseverance against all odds. As an entrepreneur it's likely you'll make mistakes along the way – success comes from learning from your own mistakes. I made so many mistakes that I should write a book about it next.

We encounter a few risks of entrepreneurship. The most frequent are:

- Bankruptcy
- Financial Risk
- Competitive Risks
- Environmental Risks
- Reputational Risks
- Political and Economic Risks

As entrepreneurs, we must plan wisely in terms of budgeting and show investors that we are considering risks by creating a realistic business plan. Make sure to talk to a professional if you are new to a business plan.

While the venture is also sown with risks, there's a light at the end of the tunnel. Self-confidence is the cornerstone of entrepreneurial success. By cultivating a positive mindset and taking persistent action, entrepreneurs can unleash their full potential. With unwavering self-belief, they can overcome challenges, inspire others, and navigate the ever-changing landscape of entrepreneurship. Most entrepreneurs are forced to work long hours to sign up customers, keep the money coming in, and the business doors open. Work-life balance can be very challenging for someone starting their own venture, and frankly one of the hardest things about being an entrepreneur.

Some skills are important to possess but not necessarily, depending on the type of venture you are embarking yourself into. The Top 10 Entrepreneurial Skills:

- Business Management Skills
- Communication and Listening
- Critical and Creative Thinking Skills
- Strategic Thinking and Planning Skills
- Branding, Marketing, and Networking Skills
- Entrepreneurial Skills in the Workplace
- Teamwork and Leadership Skills

While it looks like a lot, it can amount to a few classes online, or if you are committed, a couple of hours on youtube will get you up to date.

Since it's not that obvious, some women rather have two jobs. In addition to an increased income, you'll acquire new skills, broaden your social network and make new work contacts. However, working two jobs also introduces challenges, such as maintaining a healthy lifestyle and having time for friends and family despite working long hours. But if you have to take a second job, make sure it's one that pays you well and works with your schedule. Schedule other parts of your life, like time for household duties and socializing. Make sure you get enough sleep, exercise, and good nutrition so you don't physically or mentally burn out.

Having multiple streams of income can help you afford your goals. When you want to accomplish something, having money is one of the most important things. If you're trying to buy a house or car, go back to school, or even just pay off some bills, having multiple streams of income will make all of these things easier.

CHAPTER 7: RETIREMENT PLAN

Retirement planning involves determining retirement income goals and what's needed to achieve those goals.

Retirement planning includes identifying income sources, sizing up expenses, implementing a savings program, and managing assets and risk. What is one reason to plan for retirement now? Starting preparations for retirement early can provide financial security, maximize tax advantages, leverage compound interest, avoid catch-up contributions, and ensure a comfortable retirement with more options and flexibility.

This is why it is important to think about a retirement plan early on in life. Often, people who delay funding their retirement may not consider everything they are giving up in the future. By getting an early start on planning for retirement, you'll receive more financial security, peace of mind and enough funding to cover your expenses and dreams.

What is an example of a retirement plan? Examples of defined contribution plans include 401(k) plans, 403(b) plans, employee stock ownership plans, and profit-sharing plans. A Simplified Employee Pension Plan (SEP) is a relatively uncomplicated retirement savings vehicle. When you have a job, most of the employers are paying a huge part toward your retirement as a part of your income from their jobs. It's important to research the companies who will be working for and ensure they are making a sufficient contribution toward your retirement.

A retirement plan has lots of benefits for you as a woman and for your business if you own one and definitely for your employees.

Retirement plans allow you to invest now for financial security when you and your employees retire. As a bonus, you and your employees get significant tax advantages and other incentives.

The most offered is the 401k. What happens to a 401k when you quit? The Bottom Line. If you leave your job, your 401(k) will stay where it is until you decide what you want to do with it. You have several choices including leaving it where it is, rolling it over to another retirement account, or cashing it out. I suggest not cashing it out unless you are investing in a no risk higher interest product or using toward your life insurance benefits.

How much money should be in my 401k at age 30? Just as a generic outline, by age 30, you should have one times your annual salary saved. For example, if you're earning $50,000, you should have $50,000 banked for retirement. By age 40, you should have three times your annual salary already saved. By age 50, you should have six times your salary in an account. While those numbers sound great, things are not always that simple so we'll try using different calculations for different circumstances.

How do I know how much money I need to retire? This is one way to calculate how much you'll need to retire. A common rule of thumb is that if you want to leave the workforce at 60, you will need about 15 times the amount you have calculated for your annual after-tax retirement expenses. So if you estimate $60,000 per year, then you will need $900,000.

You can also follow the 3% Rule for an average retirement. If you are fairly confident you won't run out of money, begin by withdrawing 3% of your portfolio annually. Adjust based on inflation but keep an eye on the market, as well.

A few women are deciding to retire abroad lately. Retirement in the U.S. offers a predictable and familiar lifestyle, and you'll be close to your friends and family. Although, it can be expensive and lead to a boring routine, while retiring abroad can bring new and exciting experiences, a change of scenery, and a lower cost of living. Countries like the Philippines, the Islands and even various countries in the continent of Africa are also considered.

Here are simple steps my small business owner ladies can take right now to prepare for retirement in the future:

- Develop a Life Goals Plan
- Have an Exit Strategy
- Appraise the Future Value of Your Business
- Consider Your Other Assets and Investments
- Consider Your Retirement Planning Options
- Plan Your Will

Remember that for self-employed workers, setting up a retirement plan is a do-it-yourself job. There are four available plans tailored for the self-employed: one-participant 401(k), SEP IRA, SIMPLE IRA, and Keogh plan. Health savings plans (HSAs) and traditional and Roth IRAs are two more supplemental options. Please do not hesitate to consult a tax specialist and always a financial advisor.

CHAPTER 8: CAR

A vehicle has been from its birth an automobile that provided personal mobility.

It offered movement on an individual level much more effectively than did its predecessor the bicycle. Why is owning a car important for a woman? Having a car gives a woman the freedom to commute anywhere she needs to be. If you need to take a quick grocery trip you don't need to worry about the weather bogging down public transport. A car can help you facilitate many daily tasks. If you lead a busy life, a car can make your life so much easier.

What are nine immediate benefits of having a car that is your own?

- Safer Means of Transport
- Facilitates Many Tasks
- Flexibility
- Independence
- Saves Money

- More Trips
- Convenience
- Comfort
- Privacy

Some still wondered if a car is a necessity.

It feels almost too obvious to say that for most people living in the United States, owning a car or having access to one is a necessity.

Even after the pandemic tripled the number of Americans who primarily work from home, the vast majority of American workers — 68 percent — still drive to their jobs. However, buying or leasing a car should not be taken lightly. It's important to observe the 20-4-10 rule:

- 20% down — be able to pay 20% or more of the total purchase price up front.
- 4-year loan — be able to pay off the balance in 48 months or fewer.
- 10% of your income — your total monthly auto costs (including insurance, gas, maintenance, and car payments) should be 10% or less of your monthly income

Certainly having a car gives you the freedom to go where you want, when you want, without relying on public transportation or asking for a ride from someone else.

However, it is important to note that having a car also comes with responsibilities, such as maintaining the vehicle and paying for gas, insurance, and other expenses.

Which is why it is important to consider those aspects before choosing the car we want to own or lease. A car can make your daily life more convenient by allowing you to easily run errands, pick up groceries, or go to appointments without having to plan around bus or train schedules. The car should cover a need and not an object to impress society against what you can truly financially afford and maintain.

Having a car allows you to be more flexible in your schedule and make last-minute plans. Especially if you have to juggle more than one job or go to a job to your business. Driving a car is flexible in the sense that it allows individuals to travel to a wide variety of destinations at their own convenience, which is perfect to use as another stream of income if needed. Examples can be Uber or Lyft, just to cite those two companies.

A car offers a level of privacy that you don't get on public transportation. While driving a car can provide some level of privacy, there are still many ways in which privacy can be compromised while driving. The peace in mind that is offered when you possess your own transportation is also a gift as ideas may flow while you drive. Not to forget the relaxation and the assurance that you are in control of your destination.

Did women actually purchase vehicles? Only wealthy women were able to afford their own vehicles many many years ago, while the rest of women at most participated in the purchase of the vehicle. Moreover, cars needed to be comfortable as well as functional. When General Motors adopted the notion of annual styling in 1927 and then talked about a two-car family in 1929, they only confirmed that they were convinced of the efficacy of appealing to women.

Mobility was infectious, and once gained, whether as a shopping trip to buy groceries, as a means of going to church more easily, or as an escape from parents' watchful eyes, it was never forgotten and difficult to deny. To conclude, having a car will assist in the multitasking required to achieve our goals in a more efficient manner.

CHAPTER 9: HOUSE

Single women are the second largest group of homebuyers, making up 19% of all buyers in 2021, according to the National Association of Realtors (NAR). Married couples make up 60% of all buyers, while single men and unmarried couples each make just 9% of homebuyers.

Buying a house as a single woman is an exciting experience. But there are some unique challenges to consider when buying a house on your own. Let's explore what you need to know when buying a house as a single woman. There are a lot of benefits to homeownership, including wealth-building and the stability of a monthly housing payment that stays the same for as long as you're in the home. Buying a house offers economic freedom for single women contemplating retirement.

Every homeowner should have an emergency fund that has enough savings to cover three to six months of living expenses. But for single homeowners, it's especially important, since you won't have any additional income to rely on if things go south.

Why do women need a house of their own? Our society cannot really digest a single woman taking loans and owning a house when they have an easy option of getting married and living off their husbands. Also we observed sadly that's not the case.

More and more men are living off women.

Also, in a society like ours, very often women are deprived of this beautiful aspect of freedom where they may choose to live their lives on their own terms, far from the judgemental eyes of neighbors that stalk them almost everywhere; where they can be their true imperfect selves. Part of the joy of homeownership, especially as a single woman, is the feeling of freedom that comes with it. But if you take out a mortgage that stretches your budget too far, owning a home can quickly start to feel like a huge burden.

Before you make the leap into homeownership, make sure you can afford all of the responsibilities that come with it, not just the monthly payment. One rule of thumb says to set aside between 1% and 4% of your home's value each year to cover home upkeep. When looking to buy a home, set aside more money than you believe you need, and take time to learn how your various expenses will change throughout the year.

The mortgage approval process with one income can be very challenging, so organize your finances properly to ease the irritating part of the lending process. It's extremely necessary to shop around for the property itself and the mortgage.

When purchasing a home, treat it as a math equation. Evaluate how much you can afford to spend per month and work backwards to get your buying budget and maintain it.

Make sure to advocate for yourself during the homebuying process. People are quick to give opinions when going through the process, but do it your way.

Homeownership isn't always the right choice for everyone. Renting comes with less responsibility and more flexibility if you move around or travel a lot. It can also be cheaper. The most important thing is to have a place to call Home. But there are a lot of benefits to homeownership. With each monthly housing payment, you'll be building equity in your home. If you have a fixed-rate mortgage, you won't have to worry about your monthly payment changing dramatically (though your insurance or taxes may increase a little bit each year).

Owning a home can be a vital part of a single woman's long-term financial security. But it's important to be sure that it makes sense for your finances and your lifestyle.

Remember once you're getting married, you want to be sure to keep full ownership of your home in the event of a divorce, it's a good idea to talk with a lawyer and get a prenup.

CHAPTER 10: INVESTMENT PROPERTY

Why does a woman need an investment property?

One of the reasons why a woman may need an investment property is to take advantage of the financial advantages and long-term benefits it can offer. Investing in a property can provide a woman with a stable and reliable source of income. By purchasing a property and renting it out, she can generate rental income that can help cover the mortgage payments, property expenses, and potentially even provide passive income. This can be particularly beneficial for women looking for financial independence or additional financial security.

Furthermore, owning an investment property allows for potential appreciation in value over time. Real estate has historically shown a tendency to increase in value, and by holding onto the property for the long term, a woman can benefit from this appreciation. This can result in significant capital gains when selling the property in the future.

Additionally, an investment property can serve as a hedge against inflation. Rental income has the potential to increase over time, allowing the woman to keep up with inflation and maintain the purchasing power of her investment. This can be especially advantageous considering that the cost of living tends to rise over time. Investing in a property also provides a tangible asset that can be passed down to future generations. By building equity in the property through mortgage payments and appreciation, a woman can leave a valuable asset to her heirs. This can be a way of creating a long-lasting financial legacy for herself and her family.

Furthermore, owning an investment property can offer tax benefits. Depending on the country and specific circumstances, there may be tax deductions available for expenses related to the property, such as mortgage interest, property taxes, and maintenance costs. These deductions can help reduce the overall tax liability and increase the return on investment. When it comes to financial security and building wealth, investing in real estate can be a lucrative option for women. With numerous investment property options available, it is important to explore and understand the various choices to make informed decisions.

One common investment option for real estate is purchasing stocks, bonds, exchange-traded funds, mutual funds, or even real estate investment trusts (REITs).

These options provide an opportunity to diversify one's investment portfolio and potentially earn a steady income through dividends or property appreciation.

In addition to traditional investment options, there are other ways to invest in real estate. Online real estate investing platforms offer convenience and accessibility, allowing investors to participate in real estate opportunities remotely. These platforms provide a range of investment options, such as investing in rental properties, which can generate rental income and potential long-term appreciation.

Different types of real estate investments exist, including residential real estate, commercial real estate, raw land, real estate trust investments (REITs), and real estate crowdfunding. Each type offers unique advantages and considerations based on an investor's goals and financial capabilities. For example, residential real estate investments can provide stable rental income, while commercial real estate investments may offer higher potential returns.

Another approach to investing in real estate is to directly purchase properties for personal use or as rental properties. This allows individuals to become homeowners or landlords and potentially benefit from property appreciation and rental income. Additionally, individuals can consider house flipping, where properties are purchased, renovated, and sold for a profit.

Understanding the different financing options available is essential when investing in real estate. From conventional mortgage lenders to portfolio lenders, there are various ways to finance investment properties. These options include home equity lines of credit (HELOCs) and unsecured business lines of credit, which can provide the necessary funds to acquire and manage investment properties. Investing in an investment property offers women the opportunity to secure their financial future and build wealth. A woman may need an investment property to consider the financial advantages and long-term benefits it can provide. These include generating rental income, potential appreciation in value, protection against inflation, building equity for future generations, and potential tax benefits.

Investing in a property can be a strategic and wise financial decision for women seeking financial stability, independence, and wealth accumulation.

- Financial Independence: Owning an investment property can provide a source of passive income, allowing a woman to achieve financial independence. Rental income from the property can supplement her regular income, create a diversified investment portfolio, and potentially generate wealth in the long run.

- Retirement Planning: Investing in property can be a strategic move for retirement planning. By acquiring an investment property, a woman can secure a reliable income stream during retirement, reducing dependence on other sources of income such as pensions or social security.

- Wealth Creation: Real estate has historically proven to be a solid long-term investment. Property values tend to appreciate over time, allowing individuals to build wealth gradually. By investing in an appreciating asset like real estate, a woman can potentially increase her net worth and achieve financial stability.

- Tax Benefits: Owning an investment property also offers potential tax advantages. Deductions such as mortgage interest payments, property taxes, insurance premiums, and depreciation can help reduce taxable income, resulting in lower tax liabilities.

Now, regarding the sub-task of consulting with a financial advisor or real estate agent, it is highly recommended to seek professional guidance before making any significant investment decisions. Here's why:

- Expertise and Experience: Financial advisors and real estate agents possess specialized knowledge and experience in their respective fields. They can provide valuable insights into the local real estate market, property selection, financing options, and potential risks associated with investments.

- Customized Advice: Each individual's financial situation and investment goals may vary. A professional advisor can assess a woman's specific circumstances and provide personalized advice tailored to her needs. They can help evaluate the feasibility of investment options, analyze potential returns, and estimate associated costs.

- Risk Mitigation: Investing in real estate involves various risks, including market fluctuations, property maintenance, legal considerations, and tenant management. A financial advisor or real estate agent can assist in identifying and managing these risks effectively, minimizing potential pitfalls and optimizing investment outcomes.

- Network and Resources: Professionals in the financial and real estate industries have extensive networks and access to valuable resources. They can connect investors with mortgage lenders, property managers, legal experts, and other professionals who can facilitate a smooth investment.

Let's explore a few different types of investment properties that may be suitable for women. One of the reasons why a woman may need an investment property is to gain financial independence and build wealth. Owning an investment property can provide a source of passive income and potential long-term appreciation, offering women a means to secure their financial future.

When exploring different types of investment properties suitable for women, it is important to consider factors such as location, affordability, and potential rental demand. For example:

- Residential Rental Properties: Investing in residential properties, such as single-family homes, condominiums, or apartments, can be a great option for women. These properties can generate consistent rental income and may appeal to a wide range of tenants, including families and individuals.

- Multi-Family Properties: Investing in multi-family properties, such as duplexes or triplexes, can offer multiple rental units under one ownership. This type of investment can provide diversification and potentially higher rental income compared to single-family properties.

- Vacation Rental Properties: For women looking for alternative investment options, vacation rentals can be a lucrative choice. Owning a property in a tourist destination can generate substantial rental income during peak seasons, allowing women to reap the benefits of short-term rentals.

- Commercial Properties: Investing in commercial properties, such as office spaces, retail shops, or warehouses, can be suitable for women who are comfortable with a higher level of risk. Commercial properties usually come with longer lease terms and higher rental yields, attracting businesses as tenants.

- Real Estate Investment Trusts (REITs): If direct ownership of a property seems daunting, women can consider investing in REITs. REITs are companies that own, operate, or finance income-generating real estate. Investing in REITs provides a diversified portfolio of properties and the potential for regular income through dividends.

Ultimately, the choice of investment property will depend on individual preferences, financial goals, risk tolerance, and market conditions. It is advisable to conduct thorough research, consult with real estate professionals, and consider the long-term potential and risks associated with each type of property before making an investment decision. To close this chapter, always make sure to consult with a financial advisor or real estate agent for further guidance on investing in real estate.

Final Thoughts

Conclusively, we should agree on the facts that these tools and skills will make a major difference in the outcome of our lives as a woman. Serena Williams confided in an interview for essence magazine in 2016 how she uses confidence to create her power.

Those are exactly what she said: "I guess they couldn't relate to me because I'm Black, I'm strong, I'm powerful and I'm confident. My arms might not look like the girl over there or my legs might not look like someone else or my butt or my body or my anything, if they don't have a problem with it then I look them in the eye and say, 'if you don't like it, I don't want you to like it. I'm not asking you to like it.' I like it and I love me and there's other people that do look like me and they have to love them and I'm not going to sit around and harp on those people that feel so negatively."

We are going to face opinions, judgements and preliminary expectations on how we should be, look and act. The main thing is to be confident enough to dismiss those comments and keep shining. Take for example Margaret Thatcher, the first female British prime minister and the longest-serving of the 20th century. As prime minister, she implemented economic policies that became known as Thatcherism. A Soviet journalist dubbed her the "Iron Lady", a nickname that became associated with her uncompromising politics and leadership style.

Her strong personality was undoubted and undisputed, even beyond the political world which is mostly led by men. Not only was she Europe's first woman prime minister, but the only British prime minister in the 20th century to win three consecutive terms until the time of her resignation. She accelerated the evolution of the British economy from statism to liberalism and became, by personality as much as achievement, the most renowned British political leader since Winston Churchill. Thatcher advocated greater independence of the individual from the state; an end to allegedly excessive government interference in the economy, including privatization of state-owned enterprises and the sale of public housing to tenants; reductions in expenditures on social services such as health care, education, and housing; limitations on the printing of money in accord with the economic doctrine of monetarism; and legal restrictions on trade unions.

The term Thatcherism came to refer not just to these policies but also to certain aspects of her ethical outlook and personal style, including moral absolutism, fierce nationalism, a zealous regard for the interests of the individual, and a combative, uncompromising approach to achieving political goals. Her personality made her connect with respected leaders like President Ronald Reagan who valued her opinions with high respect. After her retirement she was still glowing by continuing to speak and lecture, notably in the United States and Asia. She also established the Thatcher Foundation to support free enterprise and democracy, particularly in the newly liberated countries of central and eastern Europe.

A strong personality will determine the size of achievements in a woman's life, your place in the world and what you will be remembered for. Biotechnology, Kiran Mazumdar-Shaw is the founder of Biocon, a global biopharmaceutical company. She began Biocon out of a rented shed and grew it into India's largest listed biopharma firm in terms of revenue. She planned her journey and focused until she succeeded.

Biocon went public in 2004 and became the second Indian company to reach $1 billion on its first trading day. Mazumdar-Shaw is India's second wealthiest self-made woman (behind Nykaa founder Falguni Nayar), with a net worth of $2.1 billion as of February 2023, according to Forbes. Planning may appear as an unnecessary step in building ourselves but it will keep us organized and definitely successful.

Let me use the example of Rihanna, who is just 35 years old when we talk about finances. For me she is a Queen in that aspect compared to her peers with almost the same opportunities. While she didn't have the rich background nor a huge financial support to start, Rihanna works smartly. She is the youngest richest woman on my list of achievers. The superstar singer has made most of her $1.7 billion fortune from Fenty Beauty, a cosmetics line that she co-owns with luxury goods group LVMH. She also co-owns Savage X Fenty, a lingerie line, with investors. Her foundation, the Clara Lionel Foundation, raised $47 million for climate, racial justice, COVID-related relief, and other causes in 2020.

Rihanna headlined the Super Bowl LVII halftime show in 2023, revealing that she was pregnant with her second child. She has a net worth of $1.4 billion as of February 2023 and is included in Forbes' 2022 Power Women and America's Richest Self-Made Women. She took her investment seriously and mastered her finances to the max. When it comes to financial achievement, she is the one I am looking up to. Always well dressed, someone said it's not fashioned, not cute until Rihanna wears it.

Another beautiful, well dressed person I highly respect and honor is no less than my Black First Lady. Ever since she first stepped foot in the White House, Michelle Obama has been praised for her style, and has been seen by many as an inspiration for how to master dress codes, uplift up-and-coming designers, and nail workplace dressing. In 2022, however, we saw a different side to Michelle Obama, one where she was able to embrace a more casual, let's call it "cooler" look.

The former First Lady made a number of public appearances as she promoted her new book The Light We Carry – and we saw her adopt a much more fashion-forward wardrobe than she has done in the past.

From double denim to head-to-toe leather, so many sequins and even sportswear, Michelle headed on a new path with her wardrobe, away from the stuffy dress codes of politics, and into a more comfortable and more free way of dressing. She wore Ganni, Balmain, Brandon Maxwell and even animal-print Versace. It seemed like she was having more fun with fashion than ever before – and it suited her. Not that I can yet afford those brands nor that it's the goal here but we can always find our own style adapted to where we are in life and rock it!

Fashion and Beauty Queen Tory Burch used it as a business and established herself.

Founder of her namesake company, Tory Burch launched the U.S.-based clothing and fashion line in 2004. The brand now brings in $1.5 billion in sales annually. She was included in Forbes' 50 Over 50 (Lifestyle) and America's Self-Made Women lists in 2022.

Burch is also a philanthropist who launched the Tory Burch Foundation to support women entrepreneurs.

I will say business and pleasure and not because I am a sucker for her purses.

No doubt, whatever life you live today you want to maintain or exceed when you stop working.

Definitely educate yourself on all of the retirement plans out here that are guaranteed, business investment can always flip on you. Yes, when we hear of Real Estate God Zhang Xin it's hard to see that picture. She is co-founder of SOHO China, a real estate development firm in China that went public in 2007. Known as "the woman who built Beijing," she was once a factory worker, later graduating from Cambridge University with a master's degree in economic development. Zhang worked for Goldman Sachs before launching her company; she has since amassed a $2.8 billion fortune in real estate.

Did I say goals yet? Well, now you've heard it. I pretty much shared all I know with you, my ladies. Do your due diligence, research, educate yourself and definitely start working on your goals today. Everything you work on will grow and develop.

Sincerely
Your Dear, one and only Mouna M Fall

www.ingramcontent.com/pod-product-compliance
Lightning Source LLC
LaVergne TN
LVHW041539070526
838199LV00046B/1735